TRADITIONAL NURSERY RHYMES

Published in 1976 by Book Club Associates
© Book Club Associates 1976

Reprinted 1981, 1983

Picture Research by Celestine Dars

Printed in Great Britain
by Jarrold and Sons Ltd, Norwich

TRADITIONAL NURSERY RHYMES

and
CHILDREN'S VERSE

collected by
MICHAEL FOSS

designed by
LESLIE & LORRAINE GERRY

BOOK CLUB ASSOCIATES   LONDON

CONTENTS

INTRODUCTION

We speak, and by the making of words prove our humanity and show ourselves different from all other animals. The child, in the puzzling darkness of the new-born, hears the voice of the parent. The word becomes the mediator between the infant and the world. What language does childhood accept most easily? The baby must be lulled, the infant amused, and the child prepared. Nothing does these tasks so well as the rhythm of verse. Verse catches the attention of the youngest, pleases through all the early years, and plants seeds in the memory for later development. Hearing first the word-music of the lullaby, the infant learns, as if by stealth, the two great principles of rhythm and melody. The growing child passes on to the games of language, the alphabets and counting-songs, the repetitions and nonsense, using sounds for their own sake, and expressing delight in the new-found accomplishment of speech. And at last, the older child discovers in verse – in poetry – the mirror of the childhood world, seeing there all the beasts of the emotional forest, not only joy but terror too, love and hate, kindness and cruelty, hope and despair.
This book offers food for these early years, when the young find verse the most natural thing in the world, before the growing mind is stamped with the orderly and sober patterns of prose.

These verses are riches taken from the storerooms of childish apprehensions, and catch, as far as possible, the peculiar and singular nature of early experience. These are not verses *about* children (the sentimental deceptions of disappointed adults), but rather the verses *of* children, such as the voice of childhood might express if it had the adult ability to put things down on paper.

Time and forgetfulness have covered the native literature of childhood. The Victorian scholar J. O. Halliwell was one of the first to begin the patient work of rediscovery, and to him and all his followers this volume is indebted. In particular, the wise guidance of one man must be acknowledged: nobody has illuminated this private and half-remembered world better than Walter de la Mare, poet, critic and anthologist of childhood.

Michael Foss
February 1976

LULLABIES

Hush, little baby, don't say a word,
Papa's going to buy you a mocking bird.

If the mocking bird won't sing,
Papa's going to buy you a diamond ring.

If the diamond ring turns to brass,
Papa's going to buy you a looking-glass.

If the looking-glass gets broke,
Papa's going to buy you a billy-goat.

If the billy-goat runs away,
Papa's going to buy you another today.

Golden slumbers kiss your eyes,
Smiles awake you when you rise.
Sleep, pretty wantons, do not cry,
And I will sing a lullaby:
Rock them, rock them, lullaby.

Care is heavy, therefore sleep you;
You are care, and care must keep you.
Sleep, pretty wantons, do not cry,
And I will sing a lullaby:
Rock them, rock them, lullaby.

My little sweet darling, my comfort and joy,
Sing lullaby, lully;
In beauty excelling the princess of Troy;
Now, suck, child, and sleep, child, thy mother's sweet boy,
The gods bless and keep thee from cruel annoy;
Sweet baby, sing lullaby, lully.

With lullay, lullay, like a child,
Thou sleep'st too long, thou art beguiled.

My darling dear, my daisy flower,
Let me, quoth me, lie in your lap.
Lie still, quoth she, my paramour,
Lie still hardly, and take a nap.
His head was heavy, such was his hap,
All drowsy dreaming, drowned in sleep,
That of his love he took no keep,
With hey lullay, lullay, like a child,
Thou sleep'st too long, thou art beguiled.

3

Sweet and low, sweet and low,
Wind of the Western sea.
Low, low, breathe and blow,
Wind of the Western sea.
Over the rolling waters go,
Come from the dying moon, and blow,
Blow him again to me;
While my little one, while my pretty one sleeps.

Sleep and rest, sleep and rest,
Father will come to thee soon;
Rest, rest, on mother's breast,
Father will come to thee soon;
Father will come to his babe in the nest,
Silver sails all out of the west
Under the silver moon;
Sleep my little one, sleep my pretty one, sleep.

Baby, baby, naughty baby,
Hush, you squalling thing, I say.
Peace this moment, peace, or maybe
Bonaparte will pass this way.

Baby, baby, he's a giant,
Tall and black as Rouen steeple,
And he breakfasts, dines, rely on't,
Every day on naughty people.

Baby, baby, if he hears you,
As he gallops past the house,
Limb from limb at once he'll tear you,
Just as pussy tears a mouse.

And he'll beat you, beat you, beat you,
And he'll beat you all to pap,
And he'll eat you, eat you, eat you,
Every morsel snap, snap, snap.

Hide and seek, says the wind
In the shade of the woods;
Hide and seek, says the moon
To the hazel buds;
Hide and seek, says the cloud,
Star on to star;
Hide and seek, says the wave
At the harbour bar;
Hide and seek, say I
To myself, and step
Out of the dream of wake
Into the dream of sleep.

Sleep, sleep, beauty bright,
Dreaming in the joys of night;
Sleep, sleep, in thy sleep
Little sorrows sit and weep.

Sweet babe, in thy face
Soft desires I can trace,
Secret joys and secret smiles,
Little pretty infant wiles.

As thy softest limbs I feel
Smiles as of the morning steal
O'er thy cheek, and o'er thy breast
Where thy little heart doth rest.

O, the cunning wiles that creep
In thy little heart asleep.
When thy little heart doth wake,
Then the dreadful night shall break.

Hush ye, hush ye, little pet ye,
Hush ye, hush ye, do not fret ye,
The Black Douglas shall not get ye.

Hush-a-bye, baby, on the tree top,
When the wind blows the cradle will rock;
When the bough breaks the cradle will fall,
Down will come baby, cradle, and all.

Sweet baby, sleep; what ails my dear?
What ails my darling thus to cry?
Be still, my child, and lend thine ear,
To hear me sing thy lullaby.
My pretty lamb, forbear to weep;
Be still, my dear; sweet baby, sleep.

Thou blessed soul, what can'st thou fear?
What thing to thee can mischief do?
Thy God is now thy father dear,
His Holy Spouse thy mother too.
Sweet baby, then, forbear to weep;
Be still, my babe; sweet baby, sleep.

Whilst thus thy lullaby I sing,
For thee great blessings ripening be;
Thine Eldest Brother is a king,
And hath a kingdom bought for thee.
Sweet baby, then, forbear to weep;
Be still, my babe; sweet baby, sleep.

Sweet baby, sleep, and nothing fear;
For whatsoever thee offends
By thy protector threatened are,
And God and angels are thy friends.
Sweet baby, then, forbear to weep;
Be still, my babe; sweet baby, sleep.

Go to bed first,
A golden purse;
Go to bed second,
A golden pheasant;
Go to bed third,
A golden bird.

LEARNING GAMES
& RIDDLES

Thirty days hath September,
April, June and November;
All the rest have thirty-one,
Excepting February alone,
Which has but twenty-eight days clear
And twenty-nine in each leap year.

A was an apple-pie;
B bit it,
C cut it
D dealt it,
E eat it,
F fought for it,
G got it,
H had it,
I inspected it,
J jumped for it,
K kept it,
L longed for it,
M mourned for it,
N nodded at it,
O opened it,
P peeped at it,
Q quartered it,
R ran for it,
S stole it,
T took it,
U upset it,
V viewed it,
W wanted it,
X, Y, Z and ampersand
All wished for a piece in hand.

Hickory, dickory, dock,
The mouse ran up the clock.
The clock struck one,
The mouse ran down,
Hickory, dickory, dock.

Eeny, meeny, miny, mo,
Catch a nigger by his toe;
If he squeals, let him go,
Eeny, meeny, miny, mo.

Intery, mintery, cutery, corn,
Apple seed and briar thorn;
Wire, briar, limber lock,
Five geese in a flock,
Sit and sing by a spring,
O-U-T, and in again.

Tinker, tailor,
Soldier, sailor,
Rich man, poor man,
Beggarman,
Thief.

This year, Silk,
Next year, Satin,
Sometime, Cotton,
Never.   Rags.

In jumping and tumbling
We spend the whole day,
Till night by arriving
Has finished our play.

What then? One and all,
There's no more to be said,
As we tumbled all day,
So we tumble to bed.

A   was an archer and shot an arrow
B   was a big baker eating bread and buns
C   was a captain with curly hair
D   was a dreamer who rode a donkey
E   was an esquire and his elegant elephant
F   was a farmer having fun following his plough
G   was a goat and a goose was her friend
H   was a hunter and he hunted a hare
I   was an idler and he would do nothing
J   was a jovial judge who liked jumping a lot
K   was a king who made me a knight

L was a lion leaping through the leaves
M was a merchant going to the market
N was a nanny nursing a little child
O was an onion growing under an oak
P was a pig who was smoking a pipe
Q was a quarrel with two boys of the town
R was a rat who ate poor Richard's hat
S was a sheep who was sweet but silly
T was a thoughtful tinker mending a pot
U was my uncle, who had a unicorn
V is a veteran who tells of his valour
W is a watchman who is watching a witch
X was an extravagant but exact xylophone
Y was a yawning youth who did not like yachting
Z was a zigzagging zany, a silly fool.

What are little boys made of?
What are little boys made of?
Frogs and snails
And puppy-dogs' tails,
That's what little boys are made of.

What are little girls made of?
What are little girls made of?
Sugar and spice
And all that's nice,
That's what little girls are made of.

Timothy Titus took two ties
To tie two tups to two tall trees,
To terrify the terrible Thomas a Tullamees.

3 Three grey geese in a green field grazing,
Grey were the geese and green was the grazing.

I need not your needles,
They're needless to me,
For kneading of needles
Were needless, you see;
But did my neat trousers
But need to be kneed,
I then should have need
Of your needles indeed.

Round and round the rugged rock
The ragged rascal ran,
How many R's are there in that?
Now tell me if you can.

One, two,
Buckle my shoe;
Three, four,
Knock at the door;
Five, six,
Pick up sticks:
Seven, eight,
Lay them straight;
Nine, ten,
A big fat hen;

Eleven, twelve,
Dig and delve;
Thirteen, fourteen,
Maids a-courting;
Fifteen, sixteen,
Maids in the kitchen;
Seventeen, eighteen,
Maids in waiting;
Nineteen, twenty,
My plate's empty.

Little Nancy Etticoat,
With a white petticoat,
And a red nose;
She has no feet or hands,
The longer she stands,
The shorter she grows.
(answer: a lighted candle)

In marble halls as white as milk,
Lined with a skin as soft as silk,
Within a fountain crystal-clear,
A golden apple doth appear.
No doors there are to this stronghold,
Yet thieves break in and steal the gold.
(answer: an egg)

Long legs and short thighs,
Little head and no eyes.
(answer: a tongs)

Black I am and much admired,
Men may seek me till they're tired;
I weary horse and weary man,
Tell me this riddle if you can.
(answer: coal)

White bird featherless
Flew from Paradise,
Pitched on the castle wall;
Along came Lord Landless,
Took it up handless,
And rode away horseless to the King's white hall.
(answer: snow melted by the sun)

Solomon Grundy,
Born on Monday,
Christened on Tuesday,
Married on Wednesday,
Took ill on Thursday,
Worse on Friday,
Died on Saturday,
Buried on Sunday.
This was the end
Of Solomon Grundy.

This little pig went to market,
This little pig stayed at home,
This little pig had roast beef,
This little pig had none,
And this little pig cried,
Wee-wee-wee-wee-wee,
I can't find my way home.

Ring-a-ring o' roses,
A pocket full of posies,
A-tishoo, a-tishoo!
We all fall down.

January brings the snow,
Makes our feet and fingers glow.
February brings the rain,
Thaws the frozen lake again.
March brings breezes loud and shrill,
Stirs the dancing daffodil.
April brings the primrose sweet,
Scatters daisies at our feet.
May brings flocks of pretty lambs,
Skipping by their fleecy dams.
June brings tulips, lilies, roses,
Fills the children's hands with posies.
Hot July brings cooling showers,
Apricots and gillyflowers.
August brings the sheaves of corn,
Then the harvest home is borne.
Warm September brings the fruit,
Sportsmen then begin to shoot.
Fresh October brings the pheasant,
Then to gather nuts is pleasant.
Dull November brings the blast,
Then the leaves are whirling fast.
Chill December brings the sleet,
Blazing fire, and Christmas treat.

On the first of March,
The craws begin to search;
By the first of April,
They are sitting still;
By the first of May,
They're all flown away;
Crowping greedy back again,
With October's wind and rain.

Rain, rain, go away,
Come again another day.

Red sky at night,
Shepherd's delight;
Red sky in the morning,
Shepherd's warning.

When clouds appear
Like rocks and towers,
The earth's refreshed
By frequent showers.

If the oak is out before the ash,
Then we'll only have a splash;
If the ash is out before the oak,
Then we'll surely have a soak.

A farmer went trotting upon his grey mare,
Bumpety, bumpety, bump!
With his daughter behind him so rosy and fair,
Lumpety, lumpety, lump!

A raven cried, Croak! and they all tumbled down,
Bumpety, bumpety, bump!
The mare broke her knees and the farmer his crown,
Lumpety, lumpety, lump!

The mischievous raven flew laughing away,
Bumpety, bumpety, bump!
And vowed he would serve them the same the next day,
Lumpety, lumpety, lump!

GIRLS AND BOYS COME OUT TO PLAY
. Dorothy B. Wh

Girls and boys come out to play,
The moon doth shine as bright as day.
Leave your supper and leave your sleep,
And join your playfellows in the street.
Come with a whoop and come with a call,
Come with a good will or not at all.
Up the ladder and down the wall,
A ha'penny loaf will serve us all;
You find milk, and I'll find flour,
And we'll have a pudding in half an hour.

Brow bender,
Eye peeper,
Nose dreeper,
Mouth eater,
Chin chopper,
Ring the bell,
Knock at the door,
Lift up the latch,
Walk in . . .
Take a chair,
Sit by there,
How d'you do this morning?

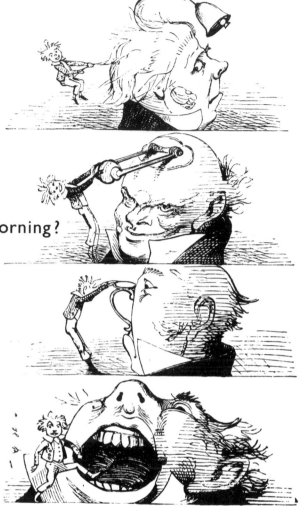

I'm the king of the castle,
Get down you dirty rascal.

Here sits the Lord Mayor,
Here sit his men,
Here sits the cockadoodle,
Here sits the hen,
Here sit the little chickens,
Here they run in,
Chin chipper, chin chopper,
Chin chopper, chin.

Round and round the garden
Like a teddy bear;
One step, two step,
Tickle you under there!

Monday's child is fair of face,
Tuesday's child is full of grace,
Wednesday's child is full of woe,
Thursday's child has far to go,
Friday's child is loving and giving,
Saturday's child works hard for its living,
But the child that is born on the Sabbath day
Is bonny and blithe, and good and gay.

MELODIES

Tell me where is fancy bred,
Or in the heart or in the head?
How begot, how nourished?
Reply, reply!
It is engendered in the eyes,
With gazing fed; and fancy dies
In the cradle where it lies.
Let us all ring fancy's knell:
I'll begin it:
Ding, dong, bell.
Ding, dong, bell.

High upon the Highlands,
and low upon Tay,
Bonnie George Campbell
rode out on a day.

Saddled and briddled
and booted rode he;
Back home came the saddle,
but never came he.

Down came his old mither,
weeping full sore,
And down came his bonny wife,
wringing her hair:

'My meadow lies green,
and my corn is unshorn,
My barn is to build
and my babe is unborn.'

Saddled and briddled
and booted rode he;
Back home came the saddle
but never came he.

Hark, hark,
The dogs do bark,
The beggars are coming to town;
Some in rags,
And some in jags,
And one in a velvet gown.

Baa, baa, black sheep,
Have you any wool?
Yes sir, yes sir,
Three bags full;
One for the master,
And one for the dame,
And one for the little boy
Who lives down the lane.

I saw three ships come sailing by,
Come sailing by, come sailing by,
I saw three ships come sailing by,
On New Year's day in the morning.

And what do you think was in them then,
Was in them then, was in them then?
And what do you think was in them then,
On New Year's day in the morning?

Three pretty girls were in them then,
Were in them then, were in them then,
Three pretty girls were in them then,
On New Year's day in the morning.

One could whistle, and one could sing,
And one could play on the violin;
Such joy there was at my wedding,
On New Year's day in the morning.

36

Mary, Mary, quite contrary,
How does your garden grow?
With silver bells and cockle shells,
And pretty maids all in a row.

Old King Cole
Was a merry old soul,
And a merry old soul was he;
He called for his pipe,
And he called for his bowl,
And he called for his fiddlers three.

Every fiddler, he had a fiddle,
And a very fine fiddle had he;
Twee tweedle dee, tweedle dee, went the fiddlers.
Oh, there's none so rare
As can compare
With King Cole and his fiddlers three.

The Queen she sits upon the strand,
Fair as lily, white as wand;
Seven billows on the sea,
Horses riding fast and free,
And bells beyond the sand.

Calico Pie,
The little birds fly
Down to the Calico tree.
There wings were blue
And they sang Tilly-loo
Till away they all flew,
And they never came back to me,
They never came back,
They never came back,
They never came back to me.

I am of Ireland,
And of the holy land
Of Ireland.

Good sir, pray I thee,
For holy charity,
Come and dance with me,
In Ireland.

Lavender's blue, dilly, dilly,
Lavender's green;
When I am king, dilly, dilly,
You shall be queen.

Call up your men, dilly, dilly,
Set them to work,
Some to the plough, dilly, dilly,
Some to the cart.

Some to make hay, dilly, dilly,
Some to thresh corn,
Whilst you and I, dilly, dilly,
Keep ourselves warm.

The Owl and the Pussy-cat went to sea
In a beautiful pea-green boat,
They took some honey, and plenty of money,
Wrapped up in a five-pound note.
The Owl looked up to the stars above,
And sang to a small guitar,
'O lovely Pussy! O Pussy, my love,
What a beautiful Pussy you are,
You are,
You are!
What a beautiful Pussy you are.

Pussy said to the Owl, 'You elegant fowl!
How charmingly sweet you sing!
O let us be married! too long we have tarried:
But what shall we do for a ring?'
They sailed away, for a year and a day,
To the land where the Bong-tree grows,
And there in a wood a Piggy-wig stood
With a ring at the end of his nose,
His nose,
His nose,
With a ring at the end of his nose.

'Dear Pig, are you willing to sell for one shilling
Your ring?' Said the Piggy, 'I will.'
So they took it away, and were married next day
By the Turkey who lives on the hill.
They dined on mince, and slices of quince,
Which they ate with a runcible spoon;
And hand in hand, on the edge of the sand,
They danced by the light of the moon,
The moon,
The moon,
They danced by the light of the moon.

When icicles hang by the wall,
And Dick the shepherd blows his nail;
And Tom bears logs into the hall,
And milk comes frozen home in pail:
When blood is nipt, and ways be foul,
Then nightly sings the staring owl,
Tu-whit to-who.
A merry note,
While greasy Joan doth keel the pot.

When all aloud the wind doth blow,
And coughing drowns the parson's saw:
The birds sit brooding in the snow,
And Marian's nose looks red and raw:
When roasted crabs hiss in the bowl,
Then nightly sings the staring owl,
Tu-whit to-who.
A merry note,
While greasy Joan doth keel the pot.

Oranges and lemons,
Say the bells of St Clement's.

You owe me five farthings,
Say the bells of St Martin's.

When will you pay me?
Say the bells of Old Bailey.

When I grow rich,
Say the bells of Shoreditch.

When will that be?
Say the bells of Stepney.

I'm sure I don't know,
Says the great bell of Bow.

Here comes a candle to light you to bed,
Here comes a chopper to chop off your head.

Come unto these yellow sands,
And then take hands:
Curtsied when you have, and kissed
The wild waves whist:
Foot it featly here and there,
And, sweet sprites, the burden bear.
Hark, hark! Bow-wow;
The watch-dogs bark: bow-wow.
Hark, hark! I hear
The strain of strutting Chanticleer
Cry Cockadiddle-do.

Lawn as white as driven snow;
Cypress black as e'er was crow;
Gloves as sweet as damask roses;
Masks for faces and for noses;
Bugle-bracelet, necklace-amber,
Perfume for a lady's chamber;
Golden quoifs and stomachers,
For my lads to give their dears;
Pins and peaking-sticks of steel;
What maids lack from head to heel:
Come buy of me, come; come buy, come buy;
Buy, lads, or else your lasses cry:
Come buy.

When daisies pied, and violets blue,
And cuckoo-buds of yellow hue:
And lady-smocks all silver white,
Do paint the meadows with delight,
The cuckoo then on every tree,
Mocks married men, for thus sings he,
Cuckoo;
Cuckoo, cuckoo: O word of fear,
Unpleasing to a married ear.

There was a jolly miller once,
Lived on the river Dee;
He worked and sang from morn till night,
No lark more blithe than he.
And this the burden of his song
Forever used to be,
I care for nobody, no, not I,
If nobody cares for me.

STORIES

Oliver Cromwell is buried and dead.
There grew an old apple tree over his head.
The apples were ripe and ready to fall.
There came an old woman and gathered them all.
Oliver rose and gave her a clop
Which made the old woman go hippity-hop.
Saddle and bridle they hang on the shelf,
If you want any more you must make it yourself.

Old Mother Hubbard
Went to the cupboard,
To fetch her poor dog a bone;
When she came there
The cupboard was bare
And so the poor dog had none.

She went to the baker's
To buy him some bread;
But when she came back
The poor dog was dead.

She went to the undertaker's
To buy him a coffin;
But when she came back
The poor dog was laughing.

She took a clean dish
To give him some tripe;
But when she came back
He was smoking a pipe.

She went to the alehouse
To get him some beer;
But when she came back
The dog sat in a chair.

She went to the tavern
For white wine and red;
But when she came back
The dog stood on his head.

She went to the fruiterer's
To buy him some fruit;
But when she came back
He was playing the flute.

She went to the tailor's
To buy him a coat;
But when she came back
He was riding a goat.

She went to the hatter's
To buy him a hat;
But when she came back
He was feeding the cat.

She went to the barber's
To buy him a wig;
But when she came back
He was dancing a jig.

She went to the cobbler's
To buy him some shoes;
But when she came back
He was reading the news.

She went to the hosier's
To buy him some hose;
But when she came back
He was dressed in his clothes.

The dame made a curtsy,
The dog made a bow;
The dame said, Your servant,
The dog said, Bow-wow.

Twinkle, twinkle, little star,
How I wonder what you are.
Up above the world so high,
Like a diamond in the sky.

When the blazing sun is gone,
When he nothing shines upon,
Then you show your little light,
Twinkle, twinkle, all the night.

St Jerome in his study kept a great big cat,
It's always in his pictures, with its feet on the mat.
Did he give it milk to drink, in a little dish?
When it came to Fridays, did he give it fish?
If I lost my little cat, I'd be sad without it;
I should ask St Jeremy what to do about it;
I should ask St Jeremy, just because of that,
For he's the only saint I know who kept a pussy cat.

Then the traveller in the dark,
Thanks you for your tiny spark,
He could not see which way to go,
If you did not twinkle so.

In the dark blue sky you keep,
And often through my curtains peep,
For you never shut your eye,
'Till the sun is in the sky.

As your bright and tiny spark,
Lights the traveller in the dark,—
Though I know not what you are,
Twinkle, twinkle, little star.

Oh, the brave old Duke of York,
He had ten thousand men;
He marched them up to the top of the hill,
And he marched them down again.
And when they were up, they were up,
And when they were down, they were down,
And when they were only half-way up,
They were neither up nor down.

Jack and Jill went up the hill
To fetch a pail of water;
Jack fell down and broke his crown,
And Jill came tumbling after.

Up Jack got, and home did trot,
As fast as he could caper,
To old Dame Dob, who patched his nob
With vinegar and brown paper.

Then Jill came in, and she did grin,
To see Jack's paper plaster;
Her mother whipt her across her knee,
For laughing at Jack's disaster.

This is the house that Jack built.

This is the malt
That lay in the house that Jack built.

This is the rat,
That ate the malt
That lay in the house that Jack built.

This is the cat,
That killed the rat,
That ate the malt
That lay in the house that Jack built.

This is the dog,
That worried the cat,
That killed the rat,
That ate the malt
That lay in the house that Jack built.

This is the cow with the crumpled horn,
That tossed the dog,
That worried the cat,
That killed the rat,
That ate the malt
That lay in the house that Jack built.

This is the maiden all forlorn,
That milked the cow with the crumpled horn,
That tossed the dog,
That worried the cat,
That killed the rat,
That ate the malt
That lay in the house that Jack built.

This is the man all tattered and torn,
That kissed the maiden all forlorn,
That milked the cow with the crumpled horn,

That tossed the dog,
That worried the cat,
That killed the rat,
That ate the malt
That lay in the house that Jack built.

This is the priest all shaven and shorn,
That married the man all tattered and torn,
That kissed the maiden all forlorn,
That milked the cow with the crumpled horn,
That tossed the dog,
That worried the cat,
That killed the rat,
That ate the malt
That lay in the house that Jack built.

This is the cock that crowed in the morn,
That waked the priest all shaven and shorn,
That married the man all tattered and torn,
That kissed the maiden all forlorn,
That milked the cow with the crumpled horn,
That tossed the dog,
That worried the cat,
That killed the rat,
That ate the malt
That lay in the house that Jack built.

This is the farmer sowing his corn,
That kept the cock that crowed in the morn,
That waked the priest all shaven and shorn,
That married the man all tattered and torn,
That kissed the maiden all forlorn,
That milked the cow with the crumpled horn,
That tossed the dog,
That worried the cat,
That killed the rat,
That ate the malt
That lay in the house that Jack built.

A frog he would a-wooing go,
Hey ho, says Rowley,
A frog he would a-wooing go,
Whether his mother would let him or no.
With a rowley, powley, gammon and spinach,
Hey ho, says Anthony Rowley.

So off he set with his opera hat,
Hey ho, says Rowley,
So off he set with his opera hat,
And on the road he met with a rat,
With a rowley, etc.

Pray Mr Rat, will you go with me?
Hey ho, says Rowley,
Pray, Mr Rat, will you go with me,
Kind Mrs Mousey for to see?
With a rowley, etc.

They came to the door of Mousey's hall,
Hey ho, says Rowley,
They gave a loud knock, and they gave a loud call.
With a rowley, etc.

Pray, Mrs Mouse, are you within?
Hey ho, says Rowley,
Oh yes, kind sirs, I'm sitting to spin.
With a rowley, etc.

Pray, Mrs Mouse, will come give us some beer,
Hey ho, says Rowley,
For Froggy and I are fond of good cheer.
With a rowley, etc.

Pray, Mr Frog, will you give us a song?
Hey ho, says Rowley,
Let it be something that's not very long.
With a rowley, etc.

58

Indeed, Mrs Mouse, replied Mr Frog,
Hey ho, says Rowley,
A cold has made me as hoarse as a dog.
With a rowley, etc.

Since you have a cold, Mr Frog, Mousey said,
Hey ho, says Rowley,
I'll sing you a song that I have just made.
With a rowley, etc.

But while they were all a-merry-making,
Hey ho, says Rowley,
A cat and her kittens came tumbling in.
With a rowley, etc.

The cat she seized the rat by the crown,
Hey ho, says Rowley,
The kittens they pulled the little mouse down.
With a rowley, etc.

This put Mr Frog in a terrible fright,
Hey ho, says Rowley,
He took up his hat and he wished them goodnight.
With a rowley, etc.

But as Froggy was crossing over a brook,
Hey ho, says Rowley,
A lily-white duck came and gobbled him up.
With a rowley, etc.

So there was an end of one, two, three,
Hey ho, says Rowley,
The rat, the mouse, and the little frog-ee.
With a rowley, etc.

London Bridge is falling down,
Falling down, falling down,
London Bridge is falling down,
My fair lady.

Build it up with wood and clay,
Wood and clay, wood and clay,
Build it up with wood and clay,
My fair lady.

Build it up with bricks and mortar,
Bricks and mortar, bricks and mortar,
Build it up with bricks and mortar,
My fair lady.

Bricks and mortar will not stay,
Will not stay, will not stay,
Bricks and mortar will not stay,
My fair lady.

Build it up with iron and steel,
Iron and steel, iron and steel,
Build it up with iron and steel,
My fair lady.

Iron and steel will bend and bow,
Bend and bow, bend and bow,
Iron and steel will bend and bow,
My fair lady.

Build it up with silver and gold,
Silver and gold, silver and gold,
Build it up with silver and gold,
My fair lady.

Silver and gold will be stolen away,
Stolen away, stolen away,
Silver and gold will be stolen away,
My fair lady.

Set a man to watch all night,
Watch all night, watch all night,
Set a man to watch all night,
My fair lady.

Give him a pipe to smoke all night,
Smoke all night, smoke all night,
Give him a pipe to smoke all night,
My fair lady.

Suppose the man should fall asleep,
Fall asleep, fall asleep,
Suppose the man should fall asleep,
My fair lady.

Maiden in the moor lay,
In the moor lay,
Seven-night full, seven-night full,
Maiden in the moor lay,
In the moor lay,
Seven nights full and a day.

Good was her meat.
What was her meat?
The cowslip and the—
The cowslip and the—
Good was her meat.
What was her meat?
The cowslip and the violet.

Good was her drink.
What was her drink?
The cold water of the—
The cold water of the—
Good was her drink.
What was her drink?
The cold water of the well-spring.

Good was her bower.
What was her bower?
The red rose and the—
The red rose and the—
Good was her bower.
What was her bower?
The red rose and the lily flower.

Little Bo-peep has lost her sheep,
And can't tell where to find them;
Leave them alone, and they'll come home,
And bring their tails behind them.

Little Bo-peep fell fast asleep,
And dreamt she heard them bleating;
But when she awoke, she found it a joke,
For they were still all fleeting.

Then up she took her little crook,
Determined for to find them;
She found them indeed, but it made her heart bleed,
For they'd left their tails behind them.

It happened one day, as Bo-peep did stray
Into a meadow hard by,
There she espied their tails side by side,
All hung on a tree to dry.

She heaved a sigh, and wiped her eye,
And over the hillocks went rambling,
And tried what she could, as a shepherdess should,
To tack again each to its lambkin.

Sing a song of sixpence,
A pocket full of rye;
Four and twenty blackbirds,
Baked in a pie.

When the pie was opened,
The birds began to sing;
Was not that a dainty dish,
To set before the king?

The king was in his counting-house,
Counting out his money;
The queen was in the parlour,
Eating bread and honey.

The maid was in the garden,
Hanging out the clothes,
There came a little blackbird,
And snapped off her nose.

WISDOM

Sticks and stones
Will break my bones,
But names will never hurt me.

When I'm dead
And in my grave,
You'll be sorry for what you called me!

Simple Simon met a pieman,
Going to the fair;
Says Simple Simon to the pieman,
Let me taste your ware.

Says the pieman to Simple Simon,
Show me first your penny;
Says Simple Simon to the pieman,
Indeed I have not any.

Simple Simon went a-fishing,
For to catch a whale;
All the water he had got
Was in his mother's pail.

Simple Simon went to look
If plums grew on a thistle;
He pricked his finger very much,
Which made poor Simon whistle.

Little Miss Muffet
Sat on a tuffet,
Eating her curds and whey;
There came a big spider,
Who sat down beside her
And frightened Miss Muffet away.

Jack Sprat could eat no fat,
His wife could eat no lean,
And so between them both, you see,
They licked the platter clean.

69

The fortunes of war I tell you plain
Are a wooden leg, or a golden chain.

If all the world were paper,
And all the sea were ink,
If all the trees were bread and cheese,
What should we do for drink?

If all our vessels ran,
If none but had a crack,
If Spanish apes eat all the grapes,
How should we do for sack?

Do not I, Time, cause nature to augment?
Do not I, Time, cause nature to decay?
Do not I, Time, cause man to be present?
Do not I, Time, take his life away?
Do not I, Time, cause death take his say?
Do not I, Time, pass his youth and age?
Do not I, Time, every thing assuage?

The world is so full of a number of things,
I'm sure we should all be as happy as kings.

71

The Queen of Hearts
She made some tarts,
All on a summer's day;
The Knave of Hearts
He stole the tarts,
And took them clean away.

The King of Hearts
Called for the tarts,
And beat the knave full sore;
The Knave of Hearts
Brought back the tarts,
And vowed he'd steal no more.

T

Tom tied a kettle to the tail of a cat,
Jill put a stone in the blind man's hat,
Bob threw his grandmother down the stairs;
And they all grew up ugly, and nobody cares.

F

For the want of a nail the shoe was lost,
For the want of a shoe the horse was lost,
For the want of a horse the rider was lost,
For the want of a rider the battle was lost,
For the want of a battle the kingdom was lost,
And all for the want of a horseshoe nail.

There's lots of ways of doing things,
As everyone supposes,
For some turn up their sleeves at work,
And some turn up their noses.

The gates of Fame are open wide,
Its halls are always full;
And some go in by the door marked Push
And some by the door marked Pull.

How many miles to Babylon?
Three score miles and ten.
Can I get there by candle-light?
Yes, and back again.
If your heels are nimble and light,
You may get there by candle-light.

Happy hearts and happy faces,
Happy play in grassy places—
That was how in ancient ages,
Children grew to kings and sages.

But the unkind and the unruly,
And the sort who eat unduly,
They must never hope for glory—
Theirs is quite a different story!

Cruel children, crying babies,
All grow up as geese and gabies,
Hated, as their age increases,
By their nephews and their nieces.

Little Tommy Tucker,
Sings for his supper:
What shall we give him?
White bread and butter.
How shall he cut it
Without a knife?
How will he be married
Without a wife?

The sword sung on the barren heath,
The sickle in the fruitful field:
The sword he sung a song of death,
But could not make the sickle yield.

Here lies our mutton-eating King
Whose word no man relies on,
Who never said a foolish thing,
Nor ever did a wise one.

The hart he loves the high wood,
The hare she loves the hill;
The knight he loves his bright sword,
The lady loves her will.

Sweet Benedict, whilst thou art young,
And know'st not yet the use of tongue,
Keep it in thrall whilst thou art free:
Imprison it or it will thee.

Goosey, goosey gander,
Whither shall I wander?
Upstairs and downstairs
And in my lady's chamber.
There I met an old man
Who would not say his prayers.
I took him by the left leg
And threw him down the stairs.

See-saw, Margery Daw,
Jacky shall have a new master;
Jacky shall have but a penny a day,
Because he can't work any faster.

Elsie Marley is grown so fine,
She won't get up to feed the swine,
But lies in bed till eight or nine.
Lazy Elsie Marley.

There was a little girl, and she had a little curl
Right in the middle of her forehead;
When she was good, she was very, very good,
And when she was bad, she was horrid.

How large unto the tiny fly
Must little things appear!—
A rosebud like a feather bed,
Its prickle like a spear;

A dewdrop like a looking-glass,
A hair like golden wire;
The smallest grain of mustard-seed
As fierce as coals of fire;

A loaf of bread, a lofty hill;
A wasp, a cruel leopard;
And specks of salt as bright to see
As lambkins to a shepherd.

My Mother said, I never should
Play with the gipsies in the wood;
If I did, she would say,
You naughty girl to disobey.

Your hair shan't curl and your shoes shan't shine,
You gipsy girl, you shan't be mine.
And my Father said that if I did
He'd rap my head with the teapot-lid.

Tom, Tom, the piper's son,
Stole a pig and away he run;

The pig was eat
And Tom was beat,
And Tom went howling down the street.

I do not love thee, Doctor Fell;
The reason why I cannot tell,
But this I know, I know full well,
I do not love thee, Doctor Fell.

Doctor Bell fell down the well
And broke his collar bone.
Doctors should attend the sick
And leave the well alone.

Doctor Foster went to Gloucester
In a shower of rain;
He stepped in a puddle
Right up to his middle,
And never went there again.

There was an old woman who lived in a shoe,
She had so many children she didn't know what to do;
She gave them some broth without any bread;
She whipped them all soundly and put them to bed.

All but blind
In his chambered hole
Groves for worms
The four-clawed Mole.

All but blind
In the evening sky
The hooded Bat
Twirls softly by.

All but blind
In the burning day
The Barn-Owl blunders
On her way.

And blind as are
These three to me,
So, blind to Some-one
I must be.

Georgie Porgie, pudding and pie,
Kissed the girls and made them cry;
When the boys came out to play,
Georgie Porgie ran away.

Children picking up our bones
Will never know that these were once
As quick as foxes on the hill.

Mirror, Mirror, tell me,
Am I pretty or plain?
Or am I downright ugly
And ugly to remain?

Shall I marry a gentleman?
Shall I marry a clown?
Or shall I marry old Knives-and-Scissors
Shouting through the town?

Woe's me, woe's me,
The acorn's not yet
Fallen from the tree
That's to grow the wood,
That's to make the cradle,
That's to rock the bairn,
That's to grow a man,
That's to lay me.

Thy Friendship oft has made my heart to ake:
Do be my Enemy for Friendship's sake.

Don't care didn't care,
Don't care was wild:
Don't care stole plum and pear
Like any beggar's child.

Don't care was made to care,
Don't care was hung:
Don't care was put in a pot
And boiled till he was done.

There was a naughty boy,
A naughty boy was he,
He would not stop at home,
He could not quiet be—
He took
In his knapsack
A book
Full of vowels
And a shirt
With some towels,
A slight cap
For night cap,
A hair brush,
Comb ditto,
New stockings—
For old ones
Would split O!
This knapsack
Tight at 's back
He rivetted close
And followed his nose
To the North,
To the North,
And followed his nose
To the North.

Little Jack Horner
Sat in the corner,
Eating a Christmas pie;
He put in a thumb,
And pulled out a plum,
And said, What a good boy am I.

LITTLE JACK HORNER

There was a naughty boy,
And a naughty boy was he,
He ran away to Scotland
The people for to see—
There he found
That the ground
Was as hard,
That a yard
Was as long,
That a song
Was as merry,
That a cherry
Was as red—
That lead
Was as weighty
That fourscore
Was as eighty,
That a door
Was as wooden
As in England—
So he stood in his shoes
And he wondered,
He wondered,
He stood in his shoes
And he wondered.

The bees
Sneeze and wheeze,
Scraping pollen and honey
From the lime trees.

The ants
Hurries and pants,
Storing up everything
They wants.

But the flies
Are wise;
When the cold weather comes
They dies.

What does the bee do?
Bring home honey.
And what does Father do?
Bring home money.
And what does Mother do?
Lay out the money.
And what does baby do?
Eat up the honey.

HUMOUR

Up and down the City Road,
In and out the Eagle,
That's the way the money goes,
Pop goes the weasel.

Half a pound of tuppenny rice,
Half a pound of treacle,
Mix it up and make it nice,
Pop goes the weasel.

Every night when I go out
The monkey's on the table;
Take a stick and knock it off,
Pop goes the weasel.

In a Village where I've been
They keep their Parson on a Green.
They tie him to a juniper tree,
And bring him currant bread for tea.
A jollier man I've never seen
Than the one on Parson's Green.

Spring is sprung,
De grass is riz,
I wonder where dem birdies is?

De little birds is on de wing,
Ain't dat absurd?
De little wing is on de bird!

It's raining, it's pouring,
The old man's snoring;
He went to bed,
And bumped his head,
And couldn't get up in the morning.

As I was going by Charing Cross,
I saw a black man upon a black horse;
They told me it was King Charles the First—
Oh dear, my heart was ready to burst!

'Beg parding, Mrs Harding,
Is my kitting in your garding?'
'Is your kitting in my garding?
Yes she is, and all alone,
Chewing on a mutting bone.'

The Grizzly Bear is huge and wild;
He has devoured the infant child.
The infant child is not aware
He has been eaten by the bear.

The dogs of the monks
Of St Bernard go,
To help little children
Out of the snow.

Each has a rum-bottle
Under his chin,
Tied with a little bit
Of bobbin.

OH dearest Bess
I like your dress;
Oh sweetest Liz
I like your phiz;
Oh dearest queen
I've never seen
A face more like
A soup-tureen.

WHO are you? A dirty old man.
I've always been so since the day I began.
Mother and Father were dirty before me,
Hot or cold water has never come o'er me.

There was a man, he went mad,
He jumped into a paper bag;
The paper bag was too narrow,
He jumped into a wheelbarrow;
The wheelbarrow took on fire,
He jumped into a cow byre;
The cow byre was too nasty,
He jumped into an apple pasty;
The apple pasty was too sweet,
He jumped into Chester-le-Street;
Chester-le-Street was full of stones,
He fell down and broke his bones.

Rutterkin is come unto our town
In a cloak without coat or gown,
Save a ragged hood to cover his crown,
Like a rutter hoyda.

Rutterkin can speak no English,
His tongue runneth all on buttered fish,
Besmeared with grease about his dish,
Like a rutter hoyda.

Rutterkin shall bring you all good luck,
A stoup of beer up at a pluck,
Till his brain be as wise as a duck,
Like a rutter hoyda.

Three jolly gentlemen,
In coats of red,
Rode their horses
Up to bed.

Three jolly gentlemen,
Snored till morn,
Their horses champing
The golden corn.

Three jolly gentlemen,
At break of day,
Came clitter-clatter down the stairs
And galloped away.

I have a little cough, sir,
In my little chest, sir,
Every time I cough, sir,
It leaves a little pain, sir,
Cough, cough, cough, cough,
There it is again, sir.

If all the seas were one sea,
What a GREAT sea that would be!
If all the trees were one tree,
What a GREAT tree that would be!
And if all the axes were one axe,
What a GREAT axe that would be!
And if all the men were one man,
What a GREAT man that would be!
And if the GREAT man took the GREAT axe,
And cut down the GREAT tree,
And let it fall into the GREAT sea,
What a splish-splash that would be!

Yankee Doodle came to town,
Riding on a pony;
He stuck a feather in his cap
And called it macaroni.

I am his Highness' dog at Kew;
Pray tell me, sir, whose dog are you?

Tweedledum and Tweedledee
Agreed to have a battle,
For Tweedledum said Tweedledee
Had spoilt his nice new rattle.
Just then flew by a monstrous crow,
As big as a tar-barrel,
Which frightened both the heroes so,
They quite forgot their quarrel.

The honey bee is sad and cross
And wicked as a weasel
And when she perches on your boss
She leaves a little measle.

I wish I was a little grub
With whiskers round my tummy,
I'd climb into a honey-pot
And make my tummy gummy.

There was a king met a king
In a narrow lane.
Says this king to that king,
Where have you been?
Oh, I've been a-hunting
The buck and the doe.
Pray lend a dog to me
That I may do so.
Take the dog Greedy Guts.
What's the dog's name?
I've told you already.
Pray tell me again.
GREEDY GUTS.

When I was a little boy I lived by myself,
And all the bread and cheese I got I laid upon a shelf;
The rats and the mice they made such a strife,
I had to go to London town to buy me a wife.

The streets were so broad and the lanes were so narrow,
I was forced to bring my wife home in a wheelbarrow.
The wheelbarrow broke and my wife had a fall,
Farewell wheelbarrow, little wife and all.

Seven Sisters in patchwork cloaks
Sat in the shadow of Seven Oaks
Stringing acorns on silken strings,
Awaiting the coming of Seven Kings.

Seven years they endured their trials
And then they consulted their Seven Dials—
O it's time, it's time, it's time, they said
It's very high time that we were wed!

I won't be my father's Jack,
I won't be my mother's Jill,
I will be the fiddler's wife
And have music when I will.
T'other little tune, t'other little tune,
Prithee love, play me t'other little tune.

FANTASY

The common cormorant or shag
Lays eggs inside a paper bag,
The reason you will see no doubt—
It is to keep the lightning out.
But what these unobservant birds
Have never noticed is that herds
Of wandering bears may come with buns
And steal the bags to hold the crumbs.

Do diddle di do,
Poor Jim Jay
Got stuck fast
In Yesterday.
Squinting he was,
On cross-legs bent,
Never heeding
The wind was spent.
Round veered the weathercock,
The sun drew in—
And stuck was Jim
Like a rusty pin. . . .
We pulled and we pulled
From seven till twelve,
Jim, too frightened
To help himself.
But all in vain.
The clock struck one,
And there was Jim
A little bit gone.
At half-past five
You scarce could see
A glimpse of his flapping
Handerkerchee.
And when came noon,
And we climbed sky-high,
Jim was a speck
Slip—slipping by.
Come to-morrow,
The neighbours say,
He'll be past crying for;
Poor Jim Jay.

Ann, Ann!
Come! quick as you can!
There's a fish that TALKS
In the frying-pan.
Out of the fat,
As clear as glass,
He put up his mouth
And moaned 'Alas!'
Oh, most mournful,
'Alas, alack!'
Then turned to his sizzling,
And sank him back.

anyone lived in a pretty how town
(with up so floating many bells down)
spring summer autumn winter
he sang his didn't he danced his did.

women and men (both little and small)
cared for anyone not at all
they sowed their isn't they reaped their same
sun moon stars rain.

Three young rats with black felt hats,
Three young ducks with white straw flats,
Three young dogs with curling tails,
Three young cats with demi-veils,
Went out to walk with two young pigs
In satin vests and sorrel wigs.
But suddenly it chanced to rain
And so they all went home again.

'Tis the voice of the Lobster: I heard him declare,
'You have baked me too brown, I must sugar my hair.'
As a duck with its eyelids, so he with his nose
Trims his belt and his buttons, and turns out his toes.

I passed by his garden, and marked, with one eye,
How the Owl and the Oyster were sharing a pie;
While the Duck and the Dodo, the Lizard and Cat,
Were swimming in milk round the brim of a hat.

What a wonderful bird the frog are—
When he stand he sit almost;
When he hop he fly almost.
He ain't got no sense hardly;
He ain't got no tail hardly either.
When he sit, he sit on what he ain't got almost.

Three Spaniards dwell on Hampstead Heath:
One has a scowl and a knife in a sheath,
One twangs a guitar in the bright moonlight,
One chases a bull round a bush all night.

Rub-a-dub-dub,
Three men in a tub,
And how do you think they got there?
The butcher, the baker,
The candlestick-maker,
They all jumped out of a rotten potato,
'Twas enough to make a man stare.

I had a little husband,
No bigger than my thumb;
I put him in a pint-pot
And there I bade him drum.
I bought a little horse,
That galloped up and down:
I bridled him, and saddled him
And sent him out of town.
I gave him some garters
To garter up his hose,
And a little silk handkerchief
To wipe his pretty nose.

In winter, when the fields are white,
I sing this song for your delight.

In spring, when woods are getting green,
I'll try and tell you what I mean.

In summer, when the days are long,
Perhaps you'll understand the song.

In autumn, when the leaves are brown,
Take pen and ink, and write it down.

I sent a message to the fish:
I told them, 'This is what I wish.'

The little fishes of the sea,
They sent an answer back to me.

The little fishes' answer was
'We cannot do it, Sir, because—'

I sent to them again to say
'It will be better to obey.'

The fishes answered, with a grin,
'Why, what a temper you are in!'

I told them once, I told them twice:
They would not listen to advice.

I took a kettle large and new,
Fit for the deed I had to do.

My heart went hop, my heart went thump:
I filled the kettle at the pump.

Then someone came to me and said,
'The little fishes are in bed.'

I said to him, I said it plain,
'Then you must wake them up again.'

I said it very loud and clear:
I went and shouted in his ear.

But he was very stiff and proud:
He said 'You needn't shout so loud!'

And he was very proud and stiff:
He said 'I'd go and wake them, if—'

I took a corkscrew from the shelf:
I went to wake them up myself.

And when I found the door was locked,
I pulled and pushed and kicked and knocked.

And when I found the door was shut,
I tried to turn the handle, BUT—

The lion and the unicorn
Were fighting for the crown;
The lion beat the unicorn
All around the town.

Some gave them white bread,
And some gave them brown;
Some gave them plum cake
And drummed them out of town.

There was a lady loved a swine,
Honey, quoth she,
Pig-hog wilt thou be mine?
Hoogh, quoth he.

I'll build for thee a silver sty,
Honey, quoth she,
And in it thou shalt lie.
Hoogh, quoth he.

Pinned with a silver pin,
Honey, quoth she,
That thou may go out and in.
Hoogh, quoth he.

What did I dream? I do not know:
The fragments fly like chaff.
Yet strange, my mind was tickled so
I cannot help but laugh.

What's your name?
Pudden Tame.
What's your other?
Bread and Butter.
Where do you live?
In a sieve.
What's your number?
Cucumber.

As I was sitting in my chair,
I KNEW the bottom wasn't there,
Nor legs nor back, but I JUST SAT,
Ignoring little things like that.

King's Cross!
What shall we do?
His purple robe
Is rent in two!
Out of his crown
He's torn the gems!
He's thrown his sceptre
Into the Thames!
The court is shaking
In its shoe—
King's Cross!
WHAT shall we do?
Leave him alone
For a minute or two.

As I was going up the hill
I met with Jack the Piper,
And all the tunes that he could play
Was 'Tie up your petticoats tighter.'

I tied them once, I tied them twice,
I tied them three times over,
And all the songs that he could sing
Was 'Carry me safe to Dover.'

Hey diddle diddle,
The cat and the fiddle,
The cow jumped over the moon;
The little dog laughed
To see such sport,
And the dish ran away with the spoon.

JOY

'I have no name:
I am but two days old.'
What shall I call thee?
'I happy am,
Joy is my name.'
Sweet joy befall thee!

Pretty joy!
Sweet joy but two days old,
Sweet joy I call thee:
Thou dost smile,
I sing the while,
Sweet joy befall thee!

There were three sisters fair and bright,
Jennifer gentle and rosemary,
And they three loved one valiant knight.
As the dew flies over the mulberry tree.

The eldest sister let him in,
Jennifer etc.,
And barred the door with a silver pin,
As the dew etc.,

The second sister made his bed,
Jennifer etc.,
And placed soft pillows under his head,
As the dew etc.,

The youngest sister, fair and bright,
Jennifer etc.,
Was resolved for to wed with this valiant knight,
As the dew etc.,

'And if you can answer questions three,
Jennifer etc.,
O then, fair maid, I will marry with thee,
As the dew etc.,'

'What is louder than a horn,
Jennifer etc.,
And what is sharper than a thorn?
As the dew etc.,'

'Thunder is louder than an horn,
Jennifer etc.,
And hunger is sharper than a thorn,
As the dew etc.'

'What is broader than the way,
Jennifer etc.,
And what is deeper than the sea?
As the dew etc.'

'Love is broader than the way,
Jennifer etc.,
And hell is deeper than the sea,
As the dew etc.'

'And now, fair maid, I will marry thee,
Jennifer gentle and rosemary.'

The King of China's daughter
So beautiful to see
With her face like yellow water, left
Her nutmeg tree.
Her little rope for skipping
She kissed and gave it me—
Made of painted notes of singing-birds
Among the fields of tea.
I skipped across the nutmeg grove—
I skipped across the sea;
But neither sun nor moon, my dear,
Has yet caught me.
128

Ride a cock-horse to Banbury Cross,
To see a fine lady upon a white horse;
Rings on her fingers and bells on her toes,
And she shall have music wherever she goes.

As I sat under a sycamore tree,
A sycamore tree, a sycamore tree,
I looked me out upon the sea
On Christ's Sunday at morn.

I saw three ships a-sailing there,
A-sailing there, a-sailing there,
Jesu, Mary and Joseph they bare
On Christ's Sunday at morn.

Joseph did whistle and Mary did sing,
Mary did sing, Mary did sing,
And all the bells on earth did ring
For joy our Lord was born.

O they sailed in to Bethlehem,
To Bethlehem, to Bethlehem;
St Michael was the steersman,
St John sat in the horn.

And all the bells on earth did ring,
On earth did ring, on earth did ring;
'Welcome be thou Heaven's King,
On Christ's Sunday at morn.'

Came ye by the salmon fishers?
Came ye by the roperee?
Saw ye a sailor laddie
Waiting on the coast for me?

I ken where I'm going,
I ken who's going with me;
I have a lad o' my own,
Ye dare na take 'im from me.

Stockings of blue silk,
Shoes of patent leather,
Kid to tie them up,
And gold rings on his finger.

O for six o'clock!
O for seven I weary!
O for eight o'clock!
And then I'll see my dearie.

Bobby Shafto's gone to sea,
Silver buckles at his knee;
He'll come back and marry me,
Bonny Bobby Shafto.

Bobby Shafto's fat and fair,
Combing down his yellow hair;
He's my love for evermore,
Bonny Bobby Shafto.

Piping down the valleys wild,
Piping songs of pleasant glee,
On a cloud I saw a child,
And he laughing said to me:

'Pipe a song about a Lamb!'
So I piped with merry cheer.
'Piper, pipe that song again;'
So I piped: he wept to hear.

'Drop thy pipe, thy happy pipe;
Sing thy songs of happy cheer:'
So I sung the same again,
While he wept with joy to hear.

'Piper, sit thee down and write
In a book, that all may read.'
So he vanish'd from my sight,
And I pluck'd a hollow reed,

And I made a rural pen,
And I stain'd the water clear,
And I wrote my happy songs
Every child may joy to hear.

Down in yonder meadow where the green grass grows,
Pretty Polly Pillicote bleaches her clothes.
She sang, she sang, she sang, oh, so sweet,
She sang, 'Oh, come over!' across the street.
He kissed her, he kissed her, he bought her a gown,
A gown of rich cramasie out of the town.
He bought her a gown and a guinea gold ring,
A guinea, a guinea, a guinea gold ring;
Up street and down, shine the windows made of glass,
Oh, isn't Polly Pillicote a braw young lass?
Cherries in her cheeks, and ringlets in her hair,
Hear her singing 'Handy, Dandy' up and down the stair.

Who shall have my fair lady?
Who shall have my fair lady?
Who but I, who but I, who but I?
Under the leaves so green!

The fairest man
That best love can,
Danderly, danderly,
Danderly, dan,
Under the leaves so green.

O dear, what can the matter be?
Dear, dear, what can the matter be?
O dear, what can the matter be?
Johnny's so long at the fair.

He promised he'd buy me a fairing should please me,
And then for a kiss, Oh! he vowed he would tease me,
He promised he'd buy me a bunch of blue ribbons
To tie up my bonny brown hair.
And it's O dear, what can the matter be?
etc, etc.

He promised to buy me a pair of sleeve buttons,
A pair of new garters that cost him but tu'pence,
He promised he'd bring me a bunch of blue ribbons
To tie up my bonny brown hair.
And it's O dear, what can the matter be?
etc, etc.

He promised he'd bring me a basket of posies,
A garland of lilies, a garland of roses,
A little straw hat, to set off the blue ribbons
That tie up my bonny brown hair.
And it's O dear, what can the matter be?
etc, etc.

Rosy apple, lemon, or pear,
Bunch of roses she shall wear;
Gold and silver by her side,
I know who will be the bride.
Take her by her lily-white hand,
Lead her to the altar;
Give her kisses—one, two, three—
Mother's runaway daughter.

Now's the time for mirth and play,
Saturday's an holiday;
Praise to heaven unceasing yield,
I've found a lark's nest in the field.

A lark's nest, then your playmate begs
You'd spare herself and speckled eggs;
Soon she shall ascend and sing
Your praises to the eternal King.

The bailiff beareth the bell away,
The lily, the rose, the rose I lay,
The silver is white, red is the gold,
The robes they lay in fold;
The bailiff beareth the bell away,
The lily, the rose, the rose I lay;
And through the glass window
Shines the sun.
How should I love and I so young?
The bailiff beareth the bell away,
The lily, the rose, the rose I lay.

Green peas, mutton pies,
Tell me where my Jeannie lies,
And I'll be with her ere she rise,
And cuddle her to my bosom.

I love Jeannie over and over,
I love Jeannie among the clover;
I love Jeannie, and Jeannie loves me,
That's the lass that I'll go wi.

Can you make me a cambric shirt,
Parsley, sage, rosemary, and thyme,
Without any seam or needlework?
And you shall be a true lover of mine.

Can you wash it in yonder well,
Parsley, sage, rosemary, and thyme,
Where never sprung water, nor rain ever fell?
And you shall be a true lover of mine.

Can you dry it on yonder thorn,
Parsley, sage, rosemary, and thyme,
Which never bore blossom since Adam was born?
And you shall be a true lover of mine.

Now you've asked me questions three,
Parsley, sage, rosemary, and thyme,
I hope you'll answer as many of me,
And you shall be a true lover of mine.

Can you find me an acre of land,
Parsley, sage, rosemary, and thyme,
Between the salt water and the sea sand?
And you shall be a true lover of mine.

Can you plow it with a ram's horn,
Parsley, sage, rosemary, and thyme,
And sow it all over with one peppercorn?
And you shall be a true lover of mine.

Can you reap it with a sickle of leather,
Parsley, sage, rosemary, and thyme,
And bind it up with a peacock's feather?
And you shall be a true lover of mine.

When you have done and finished your work,
Parsley, sage, rosemary, and thyme,
Then come to me for your cambric shirt,
And you shall be a true lover of mine.

My proper Bess,
My pretty Bess,
Turn once again to me.
For sleepest thou, Bess,
Or wakest thou, Bess,
Mine heart it is with thee.

My daisy delectable,
My primrose commendable,
My violet amiable,
My joy inexplicable,
Now turn again to me.

Alas, I am disdained,
And as a man half maimed,
My heart is so sore pained.
I pray thee, Bess, unfeigned,
Yet come again to me.

The rose is red, the violet blue,
The gillyflower sweet, and so are you.
These are the words you bade me say
For a pair of new gloves on Easter day.

Primrose Hill is green,
Primrose Hill is yellow.
As I walked on Primrose Hill
I met a pretty fellow.
We went up the hill,
We went down the valley,
We went through the primroses
And he said, Will you marry?

He gave me a silver clasp
And a golden ring.
We sat in the primroses
And heard the thrushes sing.

The month it was April,
The day it was sunny,
I plucked him a primrose
And the moon came up like honey.

Little Lamb, who made thee?
Dost thou know who made thee?
Gave thee life, & bid thee feed
By the streams & o'er the mead;
Gave thee clothing of delight,
Softest clothing, woolly, bright;
Gave thee such a tender voice,
Making all the vales rejoice?
Little Lamb, who made thee?
Dost thou know who made thee?

Little Lamb, I'll tell thee,
Little Lamb, I'll tell thee:
He is called by thy name,
For he calls himself a Lamb.
He is meek, & he is mild;
He became a little child.
I a child, & thou a lamb,
We are called by his name.
Little Lamb, God bless thee!
Little Lamb, God bless thee!

The first day of Christmas,
My true love sent to me
A partridge in a pear tree.

The second day of Christmas,
My true love sent to me
Two turtle doves, and
A partridge in a pear tree.

The third day of Christmas,
My true love sent to me
Three French hens,
Two turtle doves, and
A partridge in a pear tree.

The fourth day of Christmas,
My true love sent to me
Four colly birds,
Three French hens,
Two turtle doves, and
A partridge in a pear tree.

The fifth day of Christmas,
My true love sent to me
Five gold rings,
Four colly birds,
Three French hens,
Two turtle doves, and
A partridge in a pear tree.

The sixth day of Christmas,
My true love sent to me
Six geese a-laying,
Five gold rings,
Four colly birds,
Three French hens,
Two turtle doves, and
A partridge in a pear tree.

The seventh day of Christmas,
My true love sent to me
Seven swans a-swimming,
Six geese a-laying,
Five gold rings,
Four colly birds,
Three French hens,
Two turtle doves, and
A partridge in a pear tree.

The eighth day of Christmas,
My true love sent to me
Eight maids a-milking,
Seven swans a-swimming,
Six geese a-laying,
Five gold rings,
Four colly birds,
Three French hens,
Two turtle doves, and
A partridge in a pear tree.

The ninth day of Christmas,
My true love sent to me
Nine drummers drumming,
Eight maids a-milking,
Seven swans a-swimming,
Six geese a-laying,
Five gold rings,
Four colly birds,
Three French hens,
Two turtle doves, and
A partridge in a pear tree.

The tenth day of Christmas,
My true love sent to me
Ten pipers piping,
Nine drummers drumming,
Eight maids a-milking,
Seven swans a-swimming,
Six geese a-laying,
Five gold rings,
Four colly birds,
Three French hens,
Two turtle doves, and
A partridge in a pear tree.

The eleventh day of Christmas,
My true love sent to me
Eleven ladies dancing,
Ten pipers piping,
Nine drummers drumming,
Eight maids a-milking,
Seven swans a-swimming,
Six geese a-laying,
Five gold rings,
Four colly birds,
Three French hens,
Two turtle doves, and
A partridge in a pear tree.

The twelfth day of Christmas,
My true love sent to me
Twelve lords a-leaping,
Eleven ladies dancing,
Ten pipers piping,
Nine drummers drumming,
Eight maids a-milking,
Seven swans a-swimming,
Six geese a-laying,
Five gold rings,
Four colly birds,
Three French hens,
Two turtle doves, and
A partridge in a pear tree.

Merry Margaret,
As midsummer flower,
Gentle as falcon,
Or hawk of the tower:
With solace and gladness,
Much mirth and no madness,
All joy and no badness;
So joyously,
So maidenly,
So womanly
Her demeaning
In every thing,
Far, far passing
That I can indite,
Or suffice to write;
Well made, well wrought,
Far may be sought
Ere that he can find
So courteous, so kind
As Merry Margaret,
This midsummer flower,
Gentle as falcon
Or hawk of the tower.

SORROW

What are heavy? Sea-sand and sorrow;
What are brief? Today and tomorrow;
What are frail? Spring blossoms and youth;
What are deep? The ocean and truth.

FEE, FIE, FOH, FUM!

I smell the blood of an Englishman:
Be he alive or be he dead,
I'll grind his bones to make my bread.

WHO lies here?

I, Johnny Dow.
Hoo, Johnny, is that you?
Aye man, but I'm dead now.

Full fathom five thy father lies;
Of his bones are coral made:
Those are pearls that were his eyes:
Nothing of him that doth fade,
But doth suffer a sea-change
Into something rich and strange.
Sea-nymphs hourly ring his knell:
Ding-dong!
Hark! now I hear them,
Ding-dong, bell!

When Sir Joshua Reynolds died,
All nature was degraded;
The king dropped a tear into the queen's ear,
And all his pictures faded.

Here lies old Fred.
It's a pity he's dead.
We would have rather
It had been his father;
Had it been his sister,
We would not have missed her;
If the whole generation,
So much better for the nation,
But since it's only Fred
Who was alive, and is dead,
There's no more to be said.

I walked abroad in a snowy day:
I ask'd the soft snow with me to play:
She play'd & she melted in all her prime,
And the winter call'd it a dreadful crime.

There was a little man, and had a little gun,
And his bullets were made of lead, lead, lead;
He went to the brook, and shot a little duck,
Right through the middle of the head, head, head.

He carried it home to his old wife Joan,
And bade her a fire for to make, make, make,
To roast the little duck he had shot in the brook,
And he'd go and fetch her the drake, drake, drake.

Ladybird, ladybird,
Fly away home,
Your house is on fire
And your children all gone;
All except one
And that's little Ann
And she has crept under
The frying-pan.

Away, birds, away,
Take a little, and leave a little,
And do not come again;
For if you do,
I will shoot you through,
And there is an end of you.

My dear, do you know,
How a long time ago,
Two poor little children,
Whose names I don't know,
Were stolen away
On a fine summer's day,
And left in a wood,
As I've heard people say.

Among the trees high
Beneath the blue sky
They plucked the bright flowers
And watched the birds fly;
Then on blackberries fed,
And strawberries red,
And when they were weary
'We'll go home,' they said.

And when it was night
So sad was their plight,
The sun it went down,
And the moon gave no light.
They sobbed and they sighed
And they bitterly cried,
And long before morning
They lay down and died.

And when they were dead,
The robins so red
Brought strawberry leaves
And over them spread;
And all the day long,
The green branches among,
They'd prettily whistle
And this was their song—
'Poor babes in the wood!
Sweet babes in the wood!
O the sad fate of
The babes in the wood!'

IN ONE ANOTHER'S ARMS THEY DYED.

Lully, lulley! lully, lulley!
The falcon hath borne my mate away!

He bare him up, he bare him down,
He bare him into an orchard brown.

In that orchard there was an hall,
That was hanged with purple and pall.

And in that hall there was a bed,
It was hanged with gold so red.

And in that bed there lieth a knight,
His woundes bleeding day and night.

And that bed's foot there lieth a hound,
Licking the blood as it runs down.

By that bed-side kneeleth a maid,
And she weepeth both night and day.

And at that bed's head standeth a stone,
CORPUS CHRISTI written thereon.

Lully, lulley! lully, lulley!
The falcon hath borne my mate away!

Sometime we sang of mirth and play,
But now our joy is gone away,
For so many fall in decay,
Saw I never:
Whither is the wealth of England gone?
The spiritual sayeth they have none,
And so many wrongfully undone
Saw I never.

Weep, weep, ye woodmen! wail;
Your hands with sorrow wring!
Your master Robin Hood lies dead,
Therefore sigh as you sing.

Here lies his primer and his beads,
His bent bow and his arrows keen,
His good sword and his holy cross:
Now cast on flowers fresh and green.

And, as they fall, shed tears and say
Well, well-a-day! well, well-a-day!
Thus cast ye flowers fresh, and sing,
And on to Wakefield take your way.

Three blind mice, see how they run!
They all ran after the farmer's wife,
Who cut off their tails with a carving knife,
Did you ever see such a thing in your life,
As three blind mice.

Six little mice sat down to spin;
Pussy passed by and she peeped in.
What are you doing, my little men?
Weaving coats for gentlemen.
Shall I come in and cut off your threads?
No, no, Miss Pussy, you'd bite off our heads.
Oh no, I'll not; I'll help you to spin.
That may be so, but you don't come in.

Who killed Cock Robin?
I, said the sparrow,
With my bow and arrow,
I killed Cock Robin.

Who saw him die?
I, said the fly,
With my little eye,
I saw him die.

Who caught his blood?
I, said the fish,
With my little dish,
I caught his blood.

Who'll make his shroud?
I, said the beetle,
With my thread and needle,
I'll make his shroud.

Who'll dig his grave?
I, said the owl,
With my pick and shovel,
I'll dig his grave.

Who'll be the parson?
I, said the rook,
With my little book,
I'll be the parson.

Who'll be the clerk?
I, said the lark,
If it's not in the dark,
I'll be the clerk.

Who'll carry the link?
I, said the linnet,
I'll fetch it in a minute,
I'll carry the link.

Who'll be chief mourner?
I, said the dove,
I mourn for my love,
I'll be chief mourner.

Who'll carry the coffin?
I, said the kite,
If it's not through the night,
I'll carry the coffin.

Who'll bear the pall?
We, said the wren,
Both the cock and the hen,
We'll bear the pall.

Who'll sing a psalm?
I, said the thrush,
As she sat on a bush,
I'll sing a psalm.

Who'll toll the bell?
I, said the bull,
Because I can pull,
I'll toll the bell.

All the birds of the air
Fell a-sighing and a-sobbing,
When they heard the bell toll
For poor Cock Robin.

O rose, thou art sick!
The invisible worm
That flies in the night,
In the howling storm,

Has found out thy bed
Of crimson joy,
And his dark secret love
Does thy life destroy.

The north wind doth blow,
And we shall have snow,
And what will poor Robin do then?
Poor thing.
He'll sit in a barn,
And keep himself warm,
And hide his head under his wing.
Poor thing.

How should I your true love know
From another one?
By his cockle hat and staff,
And his sandal shoon.

He is dead and gone, lady,
He is dead and gone;
At his head a grass-green turf,
At his heels a stone.

White his shroud as the mountain snow,
Larded with sweet flowers;
Which bewept to the grave did go
With true-love showers.

Here she lies, a pretty bud,
Lately made of flesh and blood:
Who, as soon, fell fast asleep,
As her little eyes did peep.
Give her strewings; but not stir
The earth, that lightly covers her.

Where have you been today, Billy, my son?
Where have you been today, my only man?
I've been a-wooing, Mother, make my bed soon,
For I'm sick at heart, and fain would lay down.

What have you ate today, Billy, my son?
What have you ate today, my only man?
I've ate eel-pie, Mother, make my bed soon,
For I'm sick at heart, and shall die before noon.

Humpty Dumpty sat on a wall,
Humpty Dumpty had a great fall.
All the king's horses,
And all the king's men,
Couldn't put Humpty together again.

MYSTERY

Beside the blaze of forty fires
Giant Grim doth sit,
Roasting a thick-wooled mountain sheep
Upon an iron spit.
Above him wheels the winter sky,
Beneath him, fathoms deep,
Lies hidden in the valley mists
A village fast asleep—
Save for one restive hungry dog
That, snuffing towards the height,
Smells Grim's broiled supper-meat, and spies
His watch-fire twinkling bright.

I saw a fishpond all on fire
I saw a house bow to a squire
I saw a parson twelve feet high
I saw a cottage near the sky
I saw a balloon made of lead
I saw two sparrows run a race
I saw two horses making lace
I saw a girl just like a cat
I saw a kitten wear a hat
I saw a man who saw these too
And said though strange they all were true.

I had a silver buckle,
I sewed it on my shoe,
And 'neath a sprig of mistletoe
I danced the evening through!

I had a bunch of cowslips,
I hid them in a grot,
In case the elves should come by night
And me remember not.

I had a yellow riband,
I tied it in my hair,
That, walking in the garden,
The birds might see it there.

I had a secret laughter,
I laughed it near the wall:
Only the ivy and the wind
May tell of it at all.

A man in the wilderness asked of me,
How many strawberries grow in the sea?
I answered him as I thought good,
As many red herrings as grow in the wood.

My mother groan'd, my father wept,
Into the dangerous world I leapt;
Helpless, naked, piping loud,
Like a fiend hid in a cloud.

Struggling in my father's hands,
Striving against my swadling bands,
Bound and weary, I thought best
To sulk upon my mother's breast.

This is the Key of the Kingdom.
In that Kingdom is a city;
In that city is a town;
In that town there is a street;
In that street there winds a lane;
In that lane there is a yard;
In that yard there is a house;
In that house there waits a room;
In that room an empty bed;
And on that bed a basket—
A basket of sweet flowers:
Of flowers, of flowers;
A basket of sweet flowers.

Flowers in a basket;
Basket on a bed;
Bed in the chamber;
Chamber in the house;
House in the weedy yard;
Yard in the winding lane;
Lane in the broad street;
Street in the high town;
Town in the city;
City in the Kingdom—
This is the Key of the Kingdom:
Of the Kingdom this is the Key.

Four and twenty tailors
Went to kill a snail,
The best man among them
Durst not touch her tail;
She put out her horns
Like a little Kyloe cow,
Run, tailors, run,
Or she'll kill you all e'en now.

Draw a pail of water
For my lady's daughter;
Her father's a king and her mother's a queen,
Her two little sisters are dressed in green,
Stamping grass and parsley,
Marigold-leaves and daisies.
One rush, two rush!
Pray thee, fine lady, come under my bush.

The Sun arises in the East,
Cloth'd in robes of blood & gold;
Swords & spears & wrath increast
All around his bosom roll'd,
Crown'd with warlike fires & raging desires.

Fair maiden white and red,
Comb me smooth, and stroke my head:
And thou shalt have some cockle bread.
Gently dip, but not too deep,
For fear thou make the golden beard to weep.
Fair maid, white and red,
Comb me smooth, and stroke my head;
And every hair, a sheaf shall be,
And every sheaf a golden tree.

The cat she walks on padded claws,
The wolf on the hills lays stealthy paws,
Feathered birds in the rain-sweet sky
At their ease in the air, flit low, flit high.

The oak's blind, tender roots pierce deep,
His green crest towers, dimmed in sleep,
Under the stars whose thrones are set
Where never prince hath journeyed yet.

I heard a horseman
Ride over the hill;
The moon shone clear,
The night was still;
His helm was silver,
And pale was he;
And the horse he rode
Was of ivory.

Someone came knocking
At my wee, small door;
Someone came knocking
I'm sure—sure—sure;
I listened, I opened,
I looked to left and right,
But nought there was a-stirring
In the still dark night;
Only the busy beetle
Tap-tapping in the wall,
Only from the forest
The screech-owl's call,
Only the cricket whistling
While the dewdrops fall,
So I know not who came knocking,
At all, at all, at all.

Gray goose and gander,
Waft your wings together,
And carry the good king's daughter
Over the one-strand river.

Father! father! where are you going?
O do not walk so fast.
Speak, father, speak to your little boy,
Or else I shall be lost.

The night was dark, no father was there;
The child was wet with dew;
The mire was deep, & the child did weep,
And away the vapour flew.

I shot an arrow into the air:
I don't know how it fell or where;
But strangely enough, at my journey's end,
I found it again in the neck of a friend.

I had a little nut tree,
Nothing would it bear
But a silver nutmeg
And a golden pear.

The King of Spain's daughter
Came to visit me,
And all for the sake
Of my little nut tree.

I skipped over the ocean,
I danced over the sea,
And all the birds in the air
Couldn't catch me.

At the edge of All the Ages
A Knight sate on his steed,
His armour red and thin with rust,
His soul from sorrow freed;
And he lifted up his visor
From a face of skin and bone,
And his horse turned head and whinnied
As the twain stood there alone.

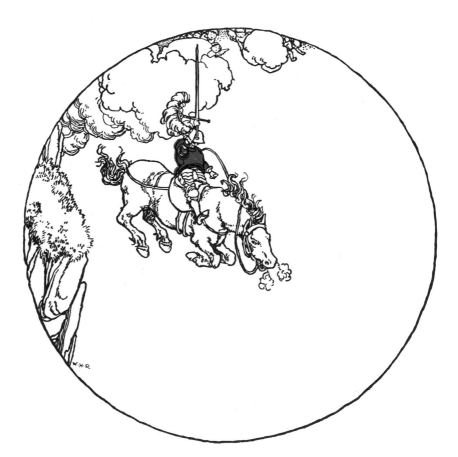

No bird above that steep of time
Sang of a livelong quest;
No wind breathed,
Rest:
'Lone for an end!' cried Knight to steed,
Loosed an eager rein—
Charged with his challenge into Space:
And quiet did quiet remain.

ACKNOWLEDGEMENTS

Walter de la Mare's poems are reprinted by
permission of the Literary Trustees of Walter de la
Mare and the Society of Authors as their
representative. The poems of Eleanor Farjeon are
from *London Rhymes* and are reprinted by
permission of the author's estate and Duckworth &
Co. The poem by e. e. cummings is reprinted by
permission of the author's estate and Granada
Publishing Ltd. The poem by Wallace Stevens is
reprinted by permission of the author's estate and
Faber & Faber Ltd.

THE ARTISTS

Photographic work by Miki Slingsby

INDEX OF FIRST LINES *(with authors in italics)*